FEEL THE FEAR

Contents

Diana Bentley

Story illustrated by
Steve May

Heinemann

In this story

 Lee   Emma

Tricky words

- scare
- scared
- can't
- very

Introduce these tricky words and help the reader when they come across them later!

Story starter

Emma and Lee are twins. They are great friends but one twin is always trying to be better than the other twin. One night, they were in their bunk beds. Emma wanted to scare Lee so she lowered a toy spider near Lee's face.

Are You Scared?

"I bet I can scare Lee," said Emma.

"Are you scared?" said E

"No, I am not scared," said Lee.

"Are you scared now?"
said Emma.

"No, I am not scared," said Lee.

"I bet you are scared now," said Emma.

"No, I am not scared,"
said Lee.
"You can't scare me."

"Now I am scared," said Lee.

"And I am scared too," said Emma.

What has scared Lee and Emma?

SCREEECH!

"We are scared," said Lee.

"We are very scared," said Emma.

Quiz

Text Detective

- Why did Emma lower the toy spider near Lee's face?
- How did Emma's trick backfire?

Word Detective

- **Phonic Focus:** Initial phonemes

  Page 6: Find a word beginning with the phoneme 'n'.
- Page 4: Find a word that means 'frightened'.
- Page 6: Find a question mark. Why is it there?

Super Speller

Read these words:

no   we

Now try to spell them!

HA! HA! HA!

Q What is a spider's favourite fairy tale?

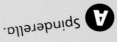 Spinderella.

13

Find out about

- Scary animals such as spiders, snakes, sharks and tigers

Tricky words

- some
- bite
- people
- scared
- very

Introduce these tricky words and help the reader when they come across them later!

Text starter

Some animals bite people and so people are scared of them. Spiders, snakes, sharks and tigers all bite people. Are you scared of these animals?

Scary Animals

This is a spider.

Some spiders bite.

Some people are scared of spiders.

Are you scared of spiders?

This is a snake.

Some snakes bite.

Some snakes bite people.

Some people are scared of snakes.

Are you scared of snakes?

This is a shark.

Some sharks bite.

Some sharks bite people.

Some people are scared of sharks.

Are you scared of sharks?

This is a tiger.

All tigers bite.

People are very scared of tigers!

Quiz

Text Detective

- Why are people very scared of tigers?
- Would you be scared of holding a snake?

Word Detective

- **Phonic Focus:** Initial phonemes

  Page 17: Find five words beginning with the phoneme 's'.
- Page 18: Find the word 'bite' twice.
- Page 16: Find two little words inside the word 'bite'.

Super Speller

Read these words:

is   of

Now try to spell them!

HA! HA! HA!

Q What do you get if you cross a pet bird with a fierce dog?

A A budgerigrrr!